Herbal Indulgences

Healing Herbal Brews, Lattes, Infusions & Other Pleasures

Darcey Blue French

Table of Contents

Herbal Infusions   **4**

Immunity Latte   5

Rose Latte   6

Turmeric Latte (Golden Milk)   8

Tulsi Coconut Latte   9

White Chocolate Kava & Lavender Latte   10

White Chocolate Latte   10

After Glow Aphrodisiac Latte   12

Palo Santo & Rose Eggnog   13

Happy Fruits   14

Clear Mind   14

Easy Digest   15

Sacred Body   15

Rooted & Grounded Morning Blend   16

Auntie Rose's Chai   17

Maple Birch Spring Tonic   18

Aphrodisiac Cacao   19

Golden Cacao   19

Craving Killer Cacao   20

Tea Infusions   **21**

Smokin Bullet Latte   22

Pocha Salted Butter Tea   23

Pumpkin Chai   24

Chai Tea   24

Peppermint & Rose Matcha Latte   25

Star of the Sea   23

Green Cardamom Chai   26

Coffee   **27**
Raspberry Maca Mocha   28
Peanut Butter Cup Mocha   29
Medicinal Mushroom Cacao   30
Pinon Coffee   32
Egg Coffee   31
Golden Coffee   33
Cherry Vanilla Latte   34

Cold & Refreshing   **35**
Salted Kefir Lassi with Lemon & Chile   36
Pine Nut & Pistachio Nut Mylks   37
Sweet Lemon Elderflower Kvass   38
Salty Ginger Beet Kvass   38
Hibiscus Lemongrass Lemonade   39
Aguas Frescas   41
Moon Water   42
Kava Kolada   43
Elderberry Ginger Shrub   45
Hawthorn Rose Shrub   45
Elderflower Shrub   45

Appendix 1 - Botanical Names   46
Appendix 2 - Resources & Where to Buy

Herbal Infusions

Immunity Latte

Immunity Latte
Serves 2

3 tbsp astragalus root
2 tbsp chaga
2 tbsp cinnamon
2 tbsp roasted dandelion root
2 tsp carob bean
1 tsp cloves
1 tsp sarsaparilla root

Mix all dried herbs together in a glass jar. Use 2-3 tbsp of dried herb for 1 quart of water. Simmer water and herbs on low for 15 min, or steep in hot water for 30 min. Strain tea from herbs and serve hot with your favorite milk and sweetener if desired. Sprinkle with cinnamon for garnish. Drink daily to support immune health.

Rose Latte

Rose Latte
serves 2

12 oz milk of choice
1 tbsp grated or slice of beet
1 tsp shatavari powder
1 tsp rose powder
1/2 tsp licorice root powder
1/2 tsp cinnamon
Pinch of vanilla bean powder
1 tbsp ghee/coconut oil
1-2 tsp honey (to taste)
2 tbsp organic rose hydrosol (rosewater)

Warm everything except the hydrosol, to piping hot in a sauce pan on medium low, do not let the milk boil.
Remove from heat and add rose hydrosol.
Blend until frothy with a stick blender or bullet.
Garnish with a sprinkle of vanilla, nutmeg and rose petals.

Turmeric Latte

Turmeric Latte (Golden Milk)
serves 2

12 oz milk of choice
2-3 tsp turmeric powder
1-2 tsp ginger powder
1/4 tsp cinnamon powder
1/8 tsp black pepper powder
1/8 tsp clove powder
1 tsp fresh ground cardamom seed
pinch of sea salt
1 tbsp coconut oil/ghee
honey to taste

squeeze of fresh orange juice
dash of cayenne or nutmeg for garnish (optional)

Warm milk, oil, and herbs in a sauce pan on medium low, until steaming hot. Add honey to taste, (or not as you like.) Whisk until well blended or whiz with a stick blender for a frothier drink. Serve hot and garnish with cayenne or nutmeg.

Tulsi Coconut Latte

Tulsi Coconut Latte
serves 2

2 tbsp tulsi (holy basil)
1 tsp ginger root
3-4 cracked cardamom pods
1 tbsp toasted coconut flakes,
unsweetened
16 oz hot water
1 can coconut milk
honey to taste

Mix herbs in a quart sized jar and pour 16 oz hot water over, cap and steep for 10 min. Add 1 can of coconut milk and honey to taste. Strain herbs from the tea and serve warm or cool as desired. Whiz with a stick blender for a frothier drink if you like!

White Chocolate Lattes

White Chocolate, Kava & Lavender Nightcap
serves 2

2 c milk of choice
2 tbsp cocoa butter, grated
1/4 tsp vanilla bean powder
1/2 tsp kava kava powder (for a stronger dose use 1 tsp, but it will change the taste)
2 tbsp lavender blossoms
1/8 tsp nutmeg, ground
1 tbsp honey
pinch of sea salt

Add milk and all herbs to a sauce pan and infuse on low heat for 10 min. (Do not let it boil. Keep your eye on it, and don't hurry it or forget it.) Remove from heat when steaming hot, and strain through a mesh strainer. Add cocoa butter, honey and infused milk back to the pan, and froth with a stick blender. Blend until cocoa butter melts and creates a luscious frothy head. Pour into mugs and serve hot with a sprinkle of nutmeg or vanilla, and a few lavender flowers.

White Chocolate Latte
serves 2

2 c milk of choice
2 tbsp cocoa butter, grated
1/4 tsp vanilla bean powder
1 tbsp honey
pinch of sea salt
2 tbsp (choose one, or more, as you like it) rose hydrosol, orange blossom hydrosol, lavender hydrosol
OR
6-8 oz brewed coffee, peppermint tea, tulsi tea, chai tea, green tea etc
Perhaps you will enjoy a combination of rose hydrosol and green tea, or orange blossom and tulsi, or peppermint and coffee. Be Creative! Be your own kitchen witch!

Add milk to a sauce pan and infuse on low heat for 10 min. (Do not let it boil. Keep your eye on it, and don't hurry it or forget it.) Remove from heat when steaming hot. Add cocoa butter, vanilla, sea salt, honey and infused milk, plus your aromatic additions back to the pan, and froth with a stick blender. Blend until cocoa butter melts and creates a luscious frothy head. Pour into mugs and serve hot with a sprinkle of nutmeg or vanilla, and a few flowers sprinkled on top.

Afterglow Latte

Afterglow Aphrodisiac Latte
serves 2

2 c milk of choice
12 oz water
1 tsp damiana
2 tbsp rose petals
2 tbsp red clover
1/2 tsp cinnamon powder
1/2 tsp cardamom powder
1/4 tsp ginger root powder
2 tsp ashwagandha powder
1 tsp maca powder
1/2 tsp licorice powder
1/4 cup chopped almonds, raw
(preferrably soaked)
6 dates, soaked and seeded
1 tbsp ghee (or coconut oil)
pinch of sea salt
(honey if desired)

Soak almonds and dates in a cup of water for 4-8 hours. (You can use them without soaking, but it is preferred for ease of assimilation to soak them before use.) Remove almond skins & date seeds, chop coarsely.

Boil water and steep damiana, rose and red clover, covered in a glass jar for 10-15 min. Strain and reserve tea, compost the herbs. Warm milk and all the herbal powders, salt and ghee in a sauce pan on low heat until hot and steaming, do not let it boil. Combine warm milk, dates, almonds, and strained tea and blend fully with a stick blender or bullet until nuts and dates are pureed smooth, and drink is frothy. Serve warm after or before lovemaking.

Note: You may want to prepare your dates, almonds and tea infusion in advance, so the warm milk and blending can be done quickly when you want to drink this with your beloved after lovemaking.

Palo Santo &
Rose Eggnog

Palo Santo, Rose and Saffron EggNog
serves 3-4

3 c half n half (or 1/2 whole milk and 1/2 cream)
4 eggs, yolks & whites separated
1/4 c maple syrup
1 tsp nutmeg
1 pinch sea salt
1/2 tsp vanilla bean paste, powder or extract
1 pinch saffron (optional)
1/4 c rose petals
1/4 c palo santo chips

Add saffron, palo santo and rose to cold half and half, and infuse on low heat for 15-20 min. Strain & Cool completely.

Beat maple syrup, vanilla, nutmeg, pinch of salt and egg yolks together until frothy. Whip into cooled infused half n half thoroughly.

In a separate dish whip egg whites into stiff peaks. Gently fold egg whites into the nog.

Sip as is, chilled, or add your favorite spirits- bourbon, rum, nocino or cognac to taste.

(Note: if you like it sweeter, add more maple syrup, or less if you want it less sweet).

Herbal Tea Blends

Happy Fruits
serves 2

1 tbsp elderberries
1 tbsp hibiscus
1 tbsp rosehips
1 tsp orange peel
2 tsp cinnamon chips
1 quart water
honey to taste

Simmer all ingredients in 1 quart of water for 5-10 minutes, or steep in hot water for 20-30 min. Strain herbs from the tea and compost, or eat in your breakfast cereal. Sweeten as desired and serve hot or cool. Make this recipe in a larger batch and store in a jar to make as desired, 2-3 tbsp dried herbs per quart of water.

Clear Mind Tea
serves 2

1 tbsp tulsi (holy basil)
1 tbsp gotu kola leaf
1 tsp rosemary
2 tsp peppermint leaf
1 tsp lemongrass
1 tsp green tea (optional)

Combine dried herbs with 1 quart hot water and steep 10 min. Serve hot or cool for an afternoon mental uplift and energizer.

Easy Digest Tea

1 tsp fennel seed
1 tsp coriander seed
1 tsp cumin seed
1/2 tsp licorice root
1 tsp ginger
2-3 cracked cardamom pods
1/2 tsp orange peel
1/2 tsp lime juice (optional)
several pinches salt (optional)

Mix all seeds and herbs together and steep in 16 oz of hot water, covered for 10-20 min. Sweeten if desired with honey, or add 1/2 tsp lime juice and several pinches of salt. Sip before or after meals to aid digestion.

Sacred Body Tea
serves 2

1 tbsp hawthorn leaf/flower
2 tbsp rose petals
1 tbsp cinnamon chips
1 tsp sarsaparilla root
1 tbsp cacao nibs or shells
1 tsp palo santo chips

Mix dried herbs together, and steep in 1 quart of hot water for 10 min. Strain and serve warm with honey and cream if desired..

15

Rooted Morning Blend

Rooted Morning Blend (A Coffee Substitute)
serves 2

2 tbsp nettles
1 tbsp chaga
1/2 tbsp roasted chicory root
1 tbsp roasted carob
1 tsp sarsaparilla root
1 tsp ginger root (optional)
1 quart water
milk of choice

In a sauce pan mix all the herbs with 1 quart of water, and simmer very gently on medium low heat for 15-20 min, covered. Remove from heat, strain herbs from tea. (You can reuse the herbs for a second batch if you like.) Sweeten as desired and add milk of choice. Serve hot or iced! (For a real treat, serve it vietnamese style with sweetened condensed milk, or sweetened coconut cream at the bottom of the glass.)

You can also make the recipe in a larger batch and store the dried herbs in a glass jar to be used as needed, 2 -3 tbsp dried herbs per quart.

Auntie Rose's Chai

**Auntie Rose's Chai
serves 2**

**2 tbsp rose petals
2 tsp shatavari root
1 tsp pink pepper
1 tbsp cinnamon
1 tbsp ginger
1/4 tsp clove
1 tsp fennel seed
6 cardamom pods,
cracked
1 star anise, cracked
(optional)
16oz hot water
milk of choice
1 tbsp honey (or to
taste)**

Mix all dried herbs
together, steep in 16
oz of hot water for 15
min. Strain, sweeten
and serve with milk of
choice.

Maple Birch Spring Tonic

Maple Birch Spring Tonic
serves 2

1 quart water
1 tbsp sweet birch bark
1 tbsp nettle leaf
1/2 tsp sassafras bark
1 tsp burdock root
1/2 tsp sarsaparilla root
1 tsp cinnamon chips
1 tbsp ginger root pieces
1 tbsp maple syrup **(or to taste)**

Simmer on LOW all ingredients in 1 quart of water for 15-20 minutes, or steep in hot water for 20-30 min. Strain herbs from the tea and compost, sweeten as desired with maple syrup and serve hot or cool. Make this recipe in a larger batch (dried herbs only) and store in a jar to make as desired, 2-3 tbsp dried herbs per quart of water.

Indulgent Cacao

Aphrodisiac Cacao
serves 2

16 oz water, hot
3 tbsp cacao powder
1 tsp hawthorn berry powder
1 tsp cinnamon powder
1 tsp maca powder
1/4 tsp vanilla bean powder
1/8 tsp chile powder or cayenne
1 tbsp honey (or more to taste)
pinch of sea salt
2 tbsp rose hydrosol (optional)

Mix all the ingredients in a sauce pan and warm gently while whisking ingredients to mix fully. Serve hot, with a dollop of whipped cream.

Golden Cacao
serves 2

1 tsp turmeric root powder
1/2 tsp cinnamon powder
1/8 tsp black pepper, ground
pinch of clove powder
pinch of cayenne powder (to taste)
2 tbsp cacao powder
1 tsp maca
pinch of sea salt
1 tbsp honey (or to taste)
16 oz hot water or milk of choice (or a combination)
1 tsp coconut oil/ghee

**Craving Killer Mexican Hot Cocoa
serves 2**

**16 oz water
4 tbsp cacao powder
1/8 tsp cayenne (or more to
taste)
1 tsp cinnamon
1/4 tsp licorice root powder
1/4 tsp vanilla bean powder
pinch of sea salt
1 whole egg beaten
2-3 tbsp heavy cream or coconut
milk**

In a saucepan mix all the herbs and spices with water and warm gently, whisky gently to mix all the ingredients. While the cocoa is heating, whisk egg and cream/coconut milk vigorously with a stick blender or beaters until foamy and frothy.

Pour foam into two mugs, then pour hot cocoa into each mug. Garnish with a dash of cinnamon or cayenne. This recipe is not sweetened, and is a more traditional way of enjoying cacao, and is very filling and kills most cravings quickly. If you wish to sweeten it with honey, you may do so before pouring cacao into the mugs.

Tea Infusions

Smokin' Bullet Latte

**Smokin Bullet Latte
serves 2**

16 oz hot water
2 tsp smoked lapsang
souchong tea
2 tsp lavender
1/2 tsp pink
peppercorns
1/2 tsp allspice,
cracked
pinch of sea salt
2 oz milk of choice
1 tbsp coconut oil or
ghee

Brew all ingredients
together in hot water/
milk for 5 minutes.
Strain, and whiz with a
stick blender or bullet
for a frothy top!
Sprinkle with vanilla
bean, cinnamon or
nutmeg powder.

22

Butter Tea & Star of the Sea

**Salted Butter Tea
serves 1**

12 oz water
1 tsp your favorite black tea, assam, ceylon, lapsang souchong etc
2 oz milk of choice
1 tbsp butter or ghee
1/4 tsp sea salt

Brew your tea in hot water and milk for 5 min. Add butter/ghee, salt, and whisk into the tea vigorously by hand or use a stick blender/bullet. (For extra interest add 1/2 tsp ginger root chips to the brew, and/or a tsp of lemon juice.)

**Star of the Sea (Seaweed Genmaicha)
serves 1**

1/2 tsp wakame seaweed
1 tsp genmaicha green tea
1/2 tsp ginger root (optional)
12 oz hot water

Mix all dried herbs in a jar or tea pot, and pour over hot water. Steep 5 min and serve warm.

Pumpkin Chai

Pumpkin Chai
serves 2
1/2 c pureed pumpkin (fresh baked is best, but canned will work)
10 oz brewed hot chai tea
4 oz warm milk of choice
1 tsp each powdered ginger, cinnamon, allspice
1/8 tsp each ground clove and nutmeg
1 tsp vanilla extract
1 tbsp molasses
1 tbsp honey or maple syrup to taste
1 tbsp ghee or coconut oil
1 egg, blended

Mix all ingredients thoroughly in a blender, or by hand with a whisk. Add more chai tea if you want it to be thinner consistency. Make sure your tea is warm when you make this and serve hot!

Chai Tea
1 tbsp black or green tea
1 tsp cinnamon
1 tbsp ginger
1 tsp fennel
4-5 cracked cardamom pods
4-6 cloves
1 tsp black pepper cracked
1 tsp licorice root
12 oz water

Simmer gently for 10-15 min. Strain well. Sweeten if desired, and add milk.

Peppermint & Rose Matcha Latte

**Peppermint & Rose Matcha Latte
serves 2**

8 oz hot water
8 oz milk of choice
1 tbsp rose petals
1 tbsp peppermint leaf
1 tbsp rose hydrosol
1/4 tsp vanilla bean powder
1-2 tsp matcha green tea
1 tbsp honey (to taste)

Brew peppermint and rose in hot water for 10 min. Strain. Add milk, honey, vanilla, matcha powder and rose hydrosol and mix well. Serve iced in the summer for an extra refreshing energizer. Add rose petals or violet flowers to an ice cube tray and freeze in cubes for a pretty garnish.

Green Cardamom Chai

Green Cardamom Chai
serves 2

2 tbsp green tea (sencha, gunpowder etc)
3 tbsp ground cardamom pods
1 tsp fennel seed
1/2 tbsp pink peppercorn
1 tbsp ginger root chips
1 tbsp peppermint
1 tbsp rose petals

1/2 tbsp lemongrass
16 oz hot water
milk of choice (as desired)
1 tbsp honey (to taste)

Mix dried herbs together and use 2 tbsp per 16 oz hot water. Steep 10 min, add milk of choice and honey. Serve warm or iced.

Coffee Beverages

Raspberry Maca Mocha

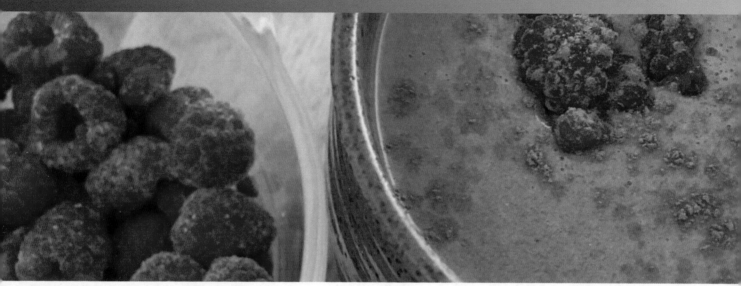

**Raspberry Maca Mocha
serves 2**

2 c hot coffee
1 tsp maca powder
1 tsp shatavari root powder
1/2 c frozen or fresh raspberries
2 tsp cacao powder
1 tbsp honey (to taste)
1 tbsp coconut oil
1/2 c milk of choice (optional)
Dash of cinnamon as garnish
pinch of sea salt

Defrost frozen raspberries. Brew your coffee, add all the herbs, fruit honey, coconut oil and whiz it all up with your blender until frothy. Add milk of choice if desired. Sprinkle with cinnamon, serve hot.

Alternative: Raspberry White Chocolate Maca Mocha
Use cocoa butter instead of coconut oil, add 1/4 tsp vanilla bean powder, and leave out the cacao powder, add 1/2 c extra milk.

Peanut Butter Cup Mocha

**Peanut Butter Cup Mocha
serves 2**

2 c hot coffee
1 tsp maca powder
1 tsp ashwagandha root powder
1 tbsp peanut butter (or use other nut butter as desired)
1 tbsp cacao powder
1 tbsp honey (to taste)
2 squares of your favorite dark chocolate
1/2 c milk of choice (optional)
pinch of sea salt

Brew your coffee, add all the herbs, nut butter, cacao powder and honey, add milk of choice if desired and whiz it all up with your blender until frothy. Place a square of dark chocolate (better if it is salted caramel filled) in the bottom of each cup. Pour the hot mocha over the chocolate to melt.

Mushroom Mocha

Medicinal Mushroom Mocha
serves 2

2 c hot coffee
2 tbsp coconut oil
2 tsp maca powder
1/2 tsp 14 Mushroom Blend powder (Mushroom Harvest)
2 tsp cacao powder
1 tbsp honey
pinch of sea salt
dash of cinnamon and pasilla ancho chile powder to garnish

Brew your coffee, add all the herbs, honey, coconut oil and whiz it all up with your blender until frothy. Add milk of choice if desired.

Egg Coffee

Egg Coffee
serves 2

2 c hot coffee
1 tbsp coconut oil/ghee
1 beaten whole, organic/free range egg
honey to taste
pinch of sea salt
dash of vanilla bean powder
milk of choice (optional)
powdered cinnamon, allspice, cacao or maca as desired (optional)

Brew your coffee, add all the herbs, honey, oil, milk (if using). You will slowly add your beaten egg to the hot coffee as you whiz it all up with your stick blender until frothy.

Piñon Pine Coffee

**Piñon Coffee
serves 2**

**2 c hot coffee
1 c milk of choice
2-3 freshly cut twigs
of piñon needles
dash of vanilla bean
powder
honey to taste**

Brew your favorite coffee as desired. Into a small sauce pan, clip piñon twigs and needles with sharp shears, (opening the needles helps release the essential oils in them) add milk and vanilla bean powder and infuse on low heat for 10-15 min. The longer you infuse the stronger the pine flavor. You can pre-infuse your milk the night before and keep it in the fridge for use the next morning. Or clip the needles into a jar of cold milk, cap and refrigerate overnight for cold infused piñon milk. Sweeten coffee as desired and add piñon infused milk as desired. You might also try this with Douglas Fir or White Fir needles in lieu of Piñon, especially if Piñon doesn't grow near you. Fresh needles are best here, as the dried lose their flavor and aroma quickly.

Golden Coffee

Golden Coffee
serves 2

1 cup golden turmeric milk
2 c hot brewed coffee
Brew both hot coffee and golden milk *(see recipe in Herbal Infusions section)*, sweeten as desired, add coconut oil/ghee, and whiz with the stick blender for a bulletproof golden coffee latte. Garnish with roses, cinnamon, red chile or nutmeg.

Cherry Vanilla Latte

Cherry Vanilla Latte
serves 2

2 c hot coffee
1 tsp shatavari or ashwagandha root powder
1/2 c frozen or fresh cherries
1 tsp vanilla bean powder
1 tbsp honey (to taste)
1 tbsp coconut oil/ghee
1/2-1 c milk of choice (optional)

dash of clove or nutmeg as garnish
pinch of sea salt

Defrost frozen cherries. Brew your coffee, add all the herbs, fruit, honey, oil, milk of choice and whiz it all up with your blender until frothy. Sprinkle with clove or nutmeg, and serve hot or iced.

34

Cold & Refreshing

Salty Kefir Lassi

Salty Kefir Lassi with Fresh Herbs, Lemon and Chile
serves 2

A large handful of favorite fresh and savory garden herbs-chives, rosemary, tagetes, calendula flowers, basil, and sage are good, even mint or lemon verbena! Use arugala for an extra spicy kick!
1/2 lemon juiced
2 chiltepin chiles, or other as you desire.
2 c plain milk kefir
1/2 tsp sea salt

Blend all the ingredients in the blender, bullet or stick blender. Pour into a big mug. Sip slowly on the porch watching the garden wake up and the sun kiss all the land with warm love.

Indulgent Nut Mylks

Pine Nut Mylk
makes 1 quart

1 c pine (pinon) nuts (shelled is best, but this works for nuts in the shell too.)
1/8 tsp sea salt
1 quart warm water
1 tsp honey (optional)
1/4 tsp vanilla bean powder (optional)

In a bullet, blender or large jar, add pine nuts, salt and 1/2 c warm water. Blend the nuts thoroughly until creamy. (If nuts have shells, grind until all the shells are broken and nuts are ground well.)
Add remainder of the water to the blender/jar, and continue blending for another minute or two. Let the milk settle for a few minutes, all the shells will sink to the bottom. Strain the milk through a few layers of cheesecloth to catch the shells.

Add vanilla and honey if desired, and refrigerate for a few hours to chill, or use immediately for coffee, cacao, or cereal. Keeps 2-3 days in the fridge.

Pistachio Nut Mylk
makes 1 quart

1/2 c shelled pistachio nuts
1/8 tsp sea salt
1 quart warm water
1 tsp honey (optional)
1/4 tsp cardamom powder (optional)
1 tsp rosewater (optional)

In a bullet, blender or large jar, add pistachios, salt and 1/2 c warm water. Blend the nuts thoroughly until creamy. Add remainder of the water to the blender/jar, and continue blending for another minute or two. Add cardamom and honey if desired, and refrigerate for a few hours to chill, or use immediately for coffee, cacao, or cereal. Keeps 2-3 days in the fridge.

Kvass (Fermented)

Sweet Lemon Elderflower Kvass
makes 1 quart

2 lemons sliced
1 c fresh elderflowers
1 quart water
handful of organic raisins
1 c sugar

Place all ingredients in a quart jar, close the jar lightly, do not tighten down. Place in a warm environment and check it daily for bubbles and fermentation. Usually this is done in about 4-7 days depending on the temperature. Tighten the lid down for half a day before serving to increase the bubbles.

Salty Ginger Beet Kvass
makes 1/2 gallon

1/2 gallon jar
2 beets chopped coarsely
3 tbsp fresh ginger, grated
1/2 gallon water
2 tbsp non iodized sea salt

Wash and chop beets, add to the jar with the salt and water and ginger. Cover and cap lightly, and let ferment in a warm place for approximately 7 days. When it is effervescent and sour, it is ready. Sip a few ounces a day, or mix in other beverages. Dilute 2 oz in cold sparkling water with lime juice or use in Bloody Marys.

Hibiscus & Lemongrass Lemonade

Hibiscus Lemongrass Lemonade
serves 2

1 quart hot water
juice of 2 or 3 lemons
1/4 c hibiscus flowers
1/4 c lemongrass
1/2 c honey (or to taste)
Sparkling water (optional)

Brew lemongrass and hibiscus in hot water for 20 min. Strain, and add lemon juice and honey. Cool for several hours. Serve over ice. For a sparkling lemonade, fill a glass half full with sparkling water, and half with lemonade.

(Try other herb combinations for lemonade i.e. rosemary peppermint, holy basil rose, lavender and chamomile etc, be creative!)

Aguas Frescas

Aguas Frescas
makes 1 quart

1 quart water or coconut water
1 c fresh fruit
1 handful fresh herbs
1 tbsp hydrosol (optional)
Ice (optional)
Blend all ingredients in 1 quart water or coconut water until very well blended. Chill and sip on a hot summers day.

Watermelon, Rose, Mint, & Aloe Vera
1 c watermelon pieces
handful of fresh peppermint
1 tbsp rose hydrosol
1/2 c aloe vera infused water

Cucumber, Mint & Lime
4 inches peeled cucumber
1 handful fresh mint leaves
juice of half a lime
1/2 c aloe water (optional)

Strawberry & Basil
1 c fresh strawberries, destemmed
1 handful fresh basil leaves

Honeydew Melon & Rosemary
1 c chopped honeydew melon
1 tbsp fresh rosemary leaves, stripped off stems

juice of 1/4 lemon

Tulsi Blueberry Sparkler
serves 2
2 c fresh holy basil leaves
1 c fresh or frozen blueberries
1 c ice
1 c water
16 oz sparkling water
In a bullet or blender, crush basil, blueberries, ice and plain water. Pour into two glasses and top with sparkling water. Add a fresh sprig of holy basil to the glass.

Aloe Vera Infused Water
1 large leaf aloe vera, peeled well
1/2 gallon water

Peel the aloe leaf very well, leaving no traces of the outer green cortex, leaving just the slimy inner leaf. (Be careful the knife can slip very easily when doing this.)
Place the inner leaf in a blender, or bullet with 2 c of water, and blend well. Add the aloe water to a 1/2 gallon jar, and top up the jar with water. Store in the refrigerator up to 1 week. Use a cup in beverages, or drink straight for extra hydration and cooling in summer.

Moon Water

Moon Water
makes 1/2 gallon

2 or 3 handfuls fresh
mugwort leaves
1 chunk of moonstone
and/or quartz crystal
1/2 gallon glass jar
1/2 gallon spring water
1 night of full moon light

Place all the ingredients
in the jar, whisper a
prayer to the full moon,
and leave the water in
the jar out in the full
moon light all night long.
Collect your water
before the sun touches it.
Strain the water from the
leaves/stones, and store
in the refrigerator. Sip
moon water on the
hottest days, or before
bed for inspiring dreams.

Kava Kava Kolada

Kava Kava Kolada
serves 4

1 can coconut milk
16 oz fresh pineapple juice
16 oz coconut water
juice of 1 lime
1/2 c kava kava powder
Warm coconut milk and kava in a sauce pan for 10-15 min. Steep covered 4-8 hrs.

Add coconut milk to coconut water, pineapple and lime juice and mix well. Blend with crushed ice, or serve on the rocks.

(Note: do not add alcohol to this recipe as Kava Kava does not mix safely with alcohol.)

Waves Photo by Christopher Sthultz/ Chrispy Photos

Mix all ingredients in a glass jar (quart sized) and infuse for two weeks covered (metal lids will corrode, use a BPA free plastic canning jar lid. Strain and compost the herbs. Save the sweet shrub in a glass vinegar jar (plastic lid). Use 1-2 tbsp of shrub in sparkling water over ice for a refreshing summer drink.

Elderberry Ginger Shrub
makes 1 pint

8 oz apple cider vinegar
8 oz raw honey
1/2 c dried or fresh elderberries
1/4 c fresh ginger root, grated

Rose & Hawthorn Shrub
makes 1 pint

8 oz apple cider vinegar
8 oz raw honey
1/2 c dried or fresh rose petals
1/4 c fresh or dried hawthorn berries

Elderflower Shrub
makes 1 pint

8 oz apple cider vinegar
8 oz raw honey
1/2 c dried or fresh elderflowers

Appendix 1 : Botanicals

allspice - *Pimenta dioica*
aloe vera - *Aloe vera*
ashwagandha - *Withania somnifera*
astragalus - *Astragalus membranaceous*
basil - *Ocimum basilicum*
birch - *Betula lenta*
black pepper - *Piper nigrum*
burdock - *Arctium lappa*
cacao - *Theobroma cacao*
cardamom - *Eletarria cardamomum*
carob - *Ceratonia siliqua*
cayenne - *Capsicum annum*
chaga - *Inodotorus obliqua*
chicory - *Chicorium intibys*
cinnamon - *Cinnamomum zeylanicum*
cloves - *Syzygium aromaticum*
coriander - *Coriandrum sativum*
cumin - *Coriandrum sativum*
damiana - *Turnera diffusa*
dandelion - *Taraxacum officials*
elder - *Sambucus nigra, S. caerulea*
fennel seed - *Foeniculum vulgare*
ginger - *Zingiber officinalis*
gotu kola - *Centella asiatica*
hawthorn - *Crategeus oxycantha*
hibiscus - *Hibiscus sabdariffa*

holy basil - *Ocimum sanctum*
kava - *Piper mythesticum*
lavender - *Lavandula officinalis*
lemongrass - *Cymbopogon citratus*
licorice - *Glycyrrhiza glabra*
maca - *Lepidium meyenii*
mugwort - *Artemisia vulgaris*
nettle - *Urtica dioica*
nutmeg - *Myristica fragrans*
orange peel - *Citrus sinensis*
palo santo - *Bursera graveolens*
peppermint - *Mentha piperita*
pink peppercorn - *Schinus molle*
pinon pine - *Pinus edulis*
red clover - *Trifolium praetense*
rose - *Rosa spp.*
rosemary - *Rosemarinus officinalis*
saffron - *Crocus sativus*
sarsaparilla - *Hemidesmus indicus*
sassafras- *Sassafras albidum*
shatavari - *Asparagus racemosus*
star anise - *Illicium verum*
turmeric - *Curcuma longa*
vanilla - *Vanilla planifolia*
wakame - *Undaria pinnatifida*

Appendix 2: Resources

Where to buy herbs and spices:

Medicinal Mushrooms - www.mushroomharvest.com

Bulk Herbs - www.mountainroseherbs.com
www.pacificbotanicals.com

Essential Oils - www.phibeearomatics.com

Kefir Grains - http://www.kefirlady.com/

Palo Santo - http://www.thirdeyewood.com/

About the Author

Darcey Blue French- Earth Medicine Guide

"I want to leave the bounds of the made world and take you out to smell wild minerals of the wet dirt, to fill your mouth with the spice of tree resin, to feed your soul with wildness, to drum your heart into a rhythm that allows YOU to hear, feel, see, sense, experience the magic and sacredness of the natural world. I want to show you how to see with more than your eyes, see with your body, your heart, your sensual nature. I want to feed the senses and bodies of my people with the holiness of Earth medicine – with the place where the earth wisdom, sacred wildness, and Spirit touches the spark of life within each heart, body and soul."

I am Darcey Blue – Devotee of the Sacred Wild. Nature is my greatest ally and teacher, the Earth my sanctuary, and seeding Sacred Wildness my purpose.

I am a rewilding woman, Earth Medicine guide, shamanic herbalist & wild crafter. The Land is my Beloved, I am a devotee of all that is wild & sacred on this beautiful, inspirited Earth.

I am here to guide to the healing wisdom and medicine that the Sacred Wild in nature hold for you, and the wisdom of spirit that is expressed within and through each of us, as medicine keepers for these transformative times. I am here to plant the seeds of a new way for our People and our Wild Communities

I work with those who are eager to learn from the Wild, Inspirited Earth, a way as old as time itself, and who are ready to take responsibility for and transform their relationship to self, body, spirit, nature, and the Earth.

I have studied plant medicine & shamanic lifeways and practices for over 10 years in the US and in in Peru. I am a Mesa Medicine Carrier, Wilderness First Responder (Jan 2017), Earth Medicine & Nature Guide and Shamanic Herbalist. It is my deep love of the wild Earth that fuels my passion for healing and teaching about sacred wilderness, spirit, deep connection and relationship with nature, and healing.

My own journey in life has been catalyzed by cultivating the ever deepening relationship with the wildness in the world, and the wildness within my own body and spirit- through the plants, the land spirits, and solitary time in wild natural places- sitting with the wild beings, wildcrafting plants, and journeying with spirit and soul.

www.whistlingstonesacredwildness.com
www.shamanaflora.com